Grandpa Lou

by Mary Ann Goldman
illustrated by Frank Sofo

Harcourt

Orlando   Boston   Dallas   Chicago   San Diego

My grandpa's name is Louis
Calhoun. Everyone calls him Lou.
I call him Grandpa Lou.

My name is Louis Calhoun, too.
Everyone calls me Louie. That way,
I know whether people are calling
Grandpa Lou or me!

I visited Grandpa Lou for lunch today. He made me split-pea soup. Grandpa Lou makes the best split-pea soup. Yum!

While we ate, Grandpa Lou told
me about his youth. I like the tales
Grandpa Lou tells about his days
as a boy. I learn a lot from them.

Grandpa Lou plays a sousaphone.
He has played it for a long time. Do
you know what a sousaphone is?

A sousaphone is a big, brass instrument. When you blow into it, the air travels through the horn to make sounds.

Have you heard of John Philip
Sousa? He wrote a lot of band
music. Grandpa Lou says that the
sousaphone was named after Sousa!

Grandpa Lou used to play his
sousaphone in a marching band.
He played music as he marched
through town.

Grandpa Lou still plays
his sousaphone. He doesn't
play in a marching band these days.
He plays in a "sitting" band.

Grandpa Lou plays with a group
of people his age. They perform
their music on a stage. I love
to hear them play!

Grandpa Lou likes to take trips.
This summer, he and Grandma will
travel through the United States.

Grandpa Lou wants to go through
as many states as he can. Today
he showed me a map. He had marked
the trip that he hopes to take.

Grandpa Lou and Grandma will
travel east on the northern route.
Then they will come home on a route
that takes them farther south.

Grandpa Lou will visit old friends
in every state he travels through.
The last time he saw some of them
was in his youth.

Sometimes I wonder what I will
be like when I grow up. I wonder
whether I will be like Grandpa Lou.
I hope so!